CHOCOLATE

From Start to Finish

Samuel G. Woods

Photographs by
Gale Zucker

BLACKBIRCH PRESS, INC.
WOODBRIDGE, CONNECTICUT

Special Thanks
The publisher would like to thank the Employees and
Family of Gertrude Hawk Chocolates for their
generous help in putting this project together.

If you would like information about Gertrude Hawk's
fundraising programs, you can call them at 1-800-822-2032.

Published by Blackbirch Press, Inc.
260 Amity Road
Woodbridge, CT 06525

e-mail: staff@blackbirch.com
Web site: www.blackbirch.com

©1999 by Blackbirch Press, Inc.
First Edition

Printed in Malaysia

10 9 8 7 6 5 4 3 2

Photo Credits: All photographs by Gale Zucker except pages 3, 18, 19, 27
(inset), 29 (silhouette), 31 (bottom right): courtesy Gertrude Hawk; page 6:
©R.L. Carlton/Photo Researchers; page 7: ©Michael J. Balick/Peter
Arnold; pages 8, 9: ©Corel Corporation; page 10: ©James L. Amos/Peter
Arnold; page 11: ©Nestle Chocolate.

Library of Congress Cataloging-in-Publication Data
Woods, Samuel G.
Chocolate from start to finish / Samuel G. Woods : photographs by Gale
Zucker—1st ed.
    p.   cm. — (Made in the U.S.A.)
    Includes bibliographical references.
    Summary: Discusses the origin, history, and ways of preparing and using
chocolate.
    ISBN 1-56711-391-5 (lib. bdg. : alk. paper)
    1. Chocolate candy Juvenile literature. 2. Candy industry Juvenile
literature. [1. Chocolate. 2. Chocolate candy. 3. Candy.] I. Zucker, Gale, ill.
II. Title. III. Series.
TX792.W66   1999
641.8'53—dc21
                                              99-20251
                                              CIP

Contents

The world is crazy about chocolate. It's America's favorite flavor. In fact, the average American eats about 12 pounds of chocolate every year! It also flavors our ice cream, our milk, our cookies—almost anything you can think of. It is given as a gift and offered for a treat. It's even packaged for special occasions such as Easter, Halloween, and Valentine's Day.

But what exactly is chocolate? And how does it actually get made?

*Solid milk chocolate bars
are always favorites.*

12 Million Pounds of Chocolate

The people at the Gertrude Hawk chocolate factory in Dunmore, Pennsylvania know a lot about making chocolate. They produce about 12 million pounds of chocolate each year! Some of it is simply molded into chocolate bars or solid chocolate pieces. Much of it is molded into unique chocolate shapes. And some of those shapes have delicious fillings in their centers.

Chocolate is not the only product the company produces. Gertrude Hawk also makes about 100,000 pounds of fudge every year!

Cacao pods.

Seeds from a Cacao Tree

Chocolate starts with cacao beans. These are actually the seeds of the cacao tree. They grow inside thick-skinned pods about the size of a coconut. The beans are protected by a white, waxy flesh.

Inside the pods are beans covered in a white, waxy flesh.

A Brief History of Chocolate

Ancient Mexican stories tell of a serpent-god named Quetzalcóatl (ketts•ah•ko•tell) who appeared in human form. In one story, this god presents the ancient people with a gift from the Garden of Paradise. The gift is a cacao tree. Quetzalcóatl shows the people how to plant the tree and harvest its fruit. He also shows them how to prepare his favorite drink: Xocolatl (chocolate).

The Olmecs

The story of chocolate-making began with the Olmec people more than 3,000 years ago. The Olmecs were the first human civilization in what is now southern Mexico and Central America. They were also probably the first people to use cacao.

Left: Sculpture of Quetzalcóatl.
Above: Olmec serpent head sculpture.

The Maya

The Olmecs passed their knowledge of cacao to the Maya. The Maya were a very advanced civilization. They built large cities and learned astronomy and mathematics. They also made drinks from cacao, which they grew on their own plantations. Scientists have found Mayan bowls and cups that date back nearly 2,000 years. These drink holders are covered with fancy illustrations about chocolate. They were used for special ceremonies.

Above: The Mayan Pyramid of the Magician.
Below: Aztec sculpture, Mexico City.

The Toltecs and Aztecs

After the Maya, other peoples of the region prized cacao. The Toltecs and the Aztecs used cacao beans for many things. It was said that Montezuma—the great Aztec emperor—loved chocolate so much that he drank 50 cups a day! And this was only one of the things he enjoyed at his regular 300-course banquets!

Roasting and Winnowing

When the beans are taken from the pod, they are fermented (aged with their natural yeasts), dried, and then roasted. At this point, they look a lot like coffee beans.

Dried cacao beans.

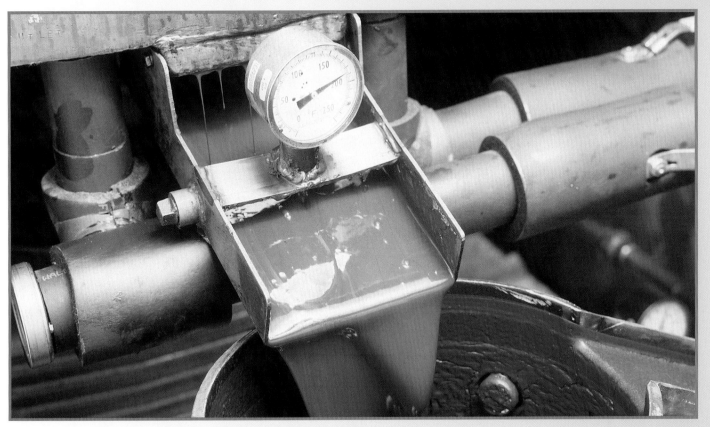

Chocolate liquor is made by heating and grinding cracked beans.

As cacao beans are roasted, their shells burst. Now the hard shells must be separated from the softer, tasty insides, called nibs. To do this, the beans are placed on a winnowing machine. This removes the beans from their shells. The nibs are ground up and turned into a thick mixture called chocolate liquor. Often, the cocoa butter (the fat) is taken out of the liquor. Later, when the liquor is used to make chocolate, some cocoa butter is blended back in.

Blending Ingredients

At the Gertrude Hawk factory, the chocolate-making process begins with blending cocoa butter together with cocoa liquor. To make milk chocolate, sugar and milk are also added. There are many other kinds of chocolate—including dark, bittersweet, semi-sweet, sugar-free, and unsweetened. Each of these requires a different blend. Some blends use no milk or sugar.

Top right: *Cocoa liquor.*
Top left: *Cocoa butter.*
Above: *Granulated sugar.*

12

The blended chocolate mixture is stored in huge stainless steel tanks. These tanks are heated to keep the chocolate in liquid form. Some tanks hold more than 60,000 pounds of chocolate!

This tank holds 60,000 lbs. of chocolate

Above: *Powdered milk.*
Right: *Supervisor Greg Zarnoski checks one of the large heated tanks.*

Large steel cylinders have holes that fill with liquid chocolate and then cool to form chocolate balls.

Pumping Chocolate

From the factory's heated tanks, liquid chocolate is pumped to many areas. Each area uses the chocolate in a different way.

At one location, liquid chocolate is poured onto a pair of large steel cylinders that are covered with holes. As the filled cylinders turn toward each other, two halves of a chocolate ball come together to form a whole.

Chocolate Side-Bar

Cacao beans were valued so highly in ancient Mexico that the Maya, Toltecs, and Aztecs used them as a form of money. A large tomato, for example, was worth 1 bean. A rabbit was priced at 10 beans. And a slave was worth 100 beans.

Great Balls of Chocolate!

When the chocolate balls have cooled, they are removed from the mold. To smooth their rough seams, they are tossed around in a huge copper drum. As they tumble, their rough edges are removed. The balls are now ready to be covered in colorful foil wrappers. Then they are sorted and packaged for sale.

Chocolate balls are tumbled to remove any rough edges.

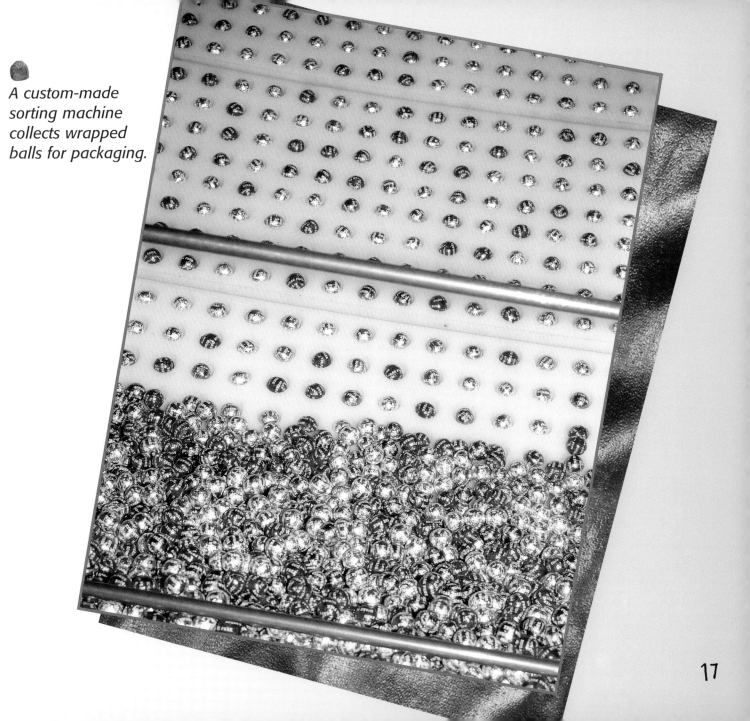

A custom-made sorting machine collects wrapped balls for packaging.

17

Sweet Success: The Gertrude Hawk Story

In 1936, Gertrude Hawk started making and selling her own chocolates. Her "factory" was the kitchen of her home in Scranton, Pennsylvania. Her dining room was her "retail store."

Ten years later, in 1946, Gertrude's son Elmer Hawk, Jr. joined the family company. By 1960, the business had grown too large for the Hawk home. Yearly sales were topping $125,000 and they were getting stronger every year. The family bought some land in a nearby town and built a factory and store. This gave them much more space for making their products.

Right: Gertrude Hawk.
Below: The orginal "factory," in Scranton.

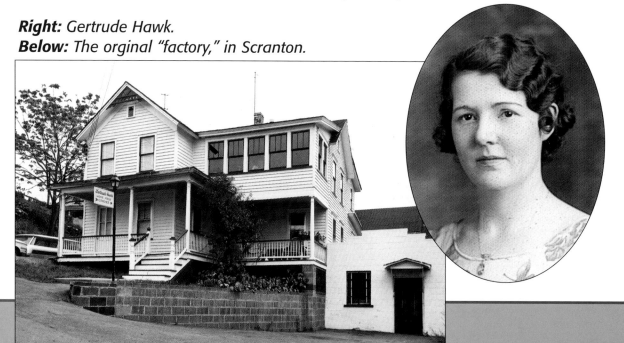

By 1971, yearly sales were more than $400,000. Gertrude's grandson David soon joined his parents in the running of the company, which now employed about 30 people. One of the company's most successful areas was

Today, Gertrude Hawk has a large, modern factory in Dunmore.

their fundraising program. With this program, Gertrude Hawk helps groups and clubs raise money by selling chocolate. As president, David also pushed the business in new and profitable directions. For the first time, the company opened multiple retail stores throughout Pennsylvania.

Today, the company's yearly sales are many millions of dollars. And, at times, the factory and stores employ up to 1,000 workers. There are more than 35 Gertrude Hawk stores in Pennsylvania and nearby areas. And the very success-ful fundraising division helps nearly 2,500 groups raise money each year.

Little Santas, Giant Bunnies

Molds of all shapes and sizes are used to make solid chocolate products. They can create everything from chocolate footballs, to huge chocolate Easter bunnies, to chocolate Santas for Christmas.

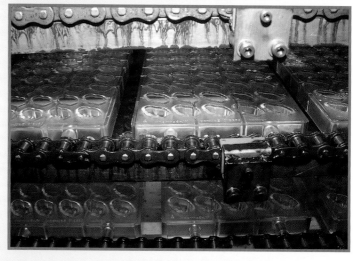

Top: Santa molds are ready to be filled.
Above and above right: Liquid chocolate is poured into the molds.
Below right: Filled molds travel through a cooling machine that hardens the chocolate.

Chocolate Santas are picked up by a special suction machine (left) and placed in plastic trays (below) before boxing.

No matter what the size or shape, molding solid chocolate means pouring it, cooling it, and removing it from the mold before wrapping.

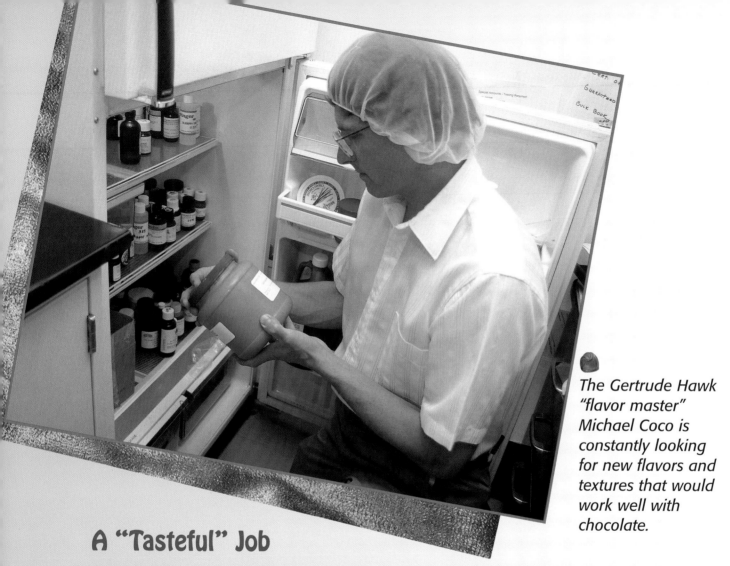

The Gertrude Hawk "flavor master" Michael Coco is constantly looking for new flavors and textures that would work well with chocolate.

A "Tasteful" Job

Developing new products is a very important part of any company. This is where people try out new ideas. It is also where they figure out how to use their technology in new and different ways.

For a chocolate company, new product development mostly means testing new flavors. But chocolate has to have more than just flavor to be appealing. It has to have a pleasing appearance. And it has to have a pleasing texture—it must feel good inside your mouth when you eat it. Making flavor, texture, and appearance come together is not easy. At Gertrude Hawk, a highly experienced "flavor master" works in a test kitchen that is part laboratory. There, he searches for new ideas by mixing flavors, extracts, and ingredients. A good knowledge of chemistry is an important tool for doing this job.

Mixing up a new batch of flavored filling for tasting.

Chocolate Side-Bar

Chocolate tastes change over time. When Gertrude Hawk started her company, the most popular fillings were peppermint, sassafrass, root beer, and molasses-coconut. Today, peanut butter is the most popular flavor.

Filling Stations

Many of Gertrude Hawk's chocolates have delicious fillings in their centers. Fillings are made from a wide variety of ingredients. And they come in many styles and textures. Some are light and creamy. Others are dense and chewy. Each kind of filling must be prepared in its own special way.

Left: A worker prepares a large pot of butter that will be used in a buttercream filling.
Far left, top: Orange cream filling, ready to use.
Far left, bottom: Cherry purée is mixed.

24

Chocolate cream filling requires special skills to make. It must be watched carefully as it mixes and must be lifted out of the machine at just the right time.

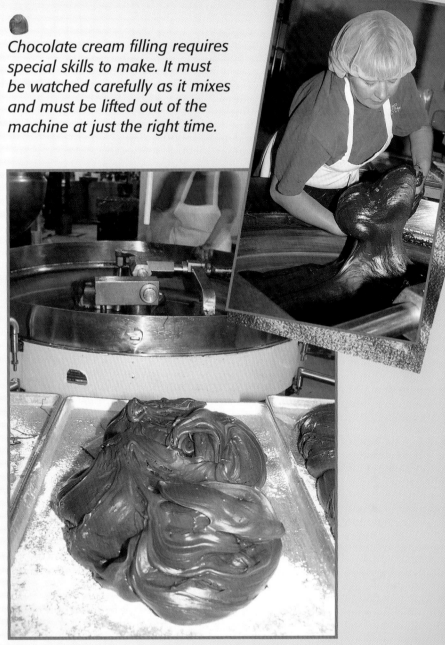

Creams are some of the most popular fillings. They are made mostly by mixing butter, sugar, and flavoring. They come in many flavors, including caramel, amaretto, hazelnut, peanut butter, orange, lemon, raspberry, strawberry, vanilla, and chocolate.

A worker cuts a chunk of coconut center from a huge tray. The coconut is placed in a machine called an extruder, which squeezes out round coconut disks (above, right) before they are coated with chocolate.

Chocolate Waterfalls

Some fillings are made from simple ingredients—such as coconut, caramel, or roasted nuts. These ingredients are often combined in different ways to create different flavor mixes, textures, and shapes.

To make coconut-filled chocolates, small mounds of coconut are squeezed out and formed by a machine. The mounds are dropped onto a moving belt that takes them to a "chocolate waterfall." As they pass under the waterfall, they are coated. This process is called "enrobing."

Coconut mounds travel on a chocolate-covered conveyer belt (a bottom coater), and are coated on top as they pass through the "chocolate waterfall."

Nuts to That!

To make caramel nut clusters, small disks of caramel are squeezed out onto a belt that is covered by nuts. The caramel sticks to the nuts as they move toward the chocolate waterfall for enrobing.

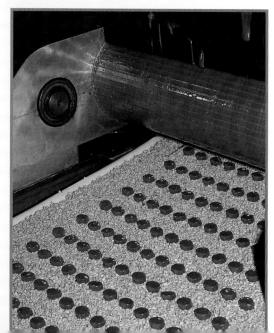

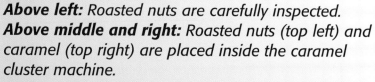

Above left: Roasted nuts are carefully inspected.
Above middle and right: Roasted nuts (top left) and caramel (top right) are placed inside the caramel cluster machine.
Right: Caramel disks are pressed out onto a bed of nuts as they move toward the chocolate waterfall.

Right: Workers quickly pick out the clusters that are not properly shaped.
Below: The clusters pass through the chocolate waterfall and are then decorated as they pass under a decorating machine.

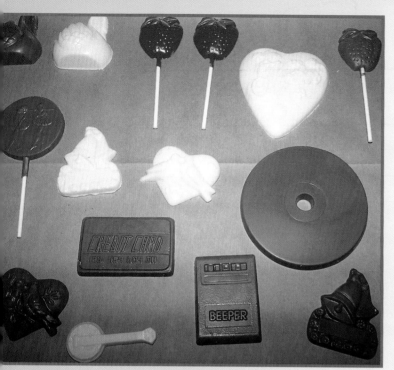

Chocolate Calculators

One of the best things about molding chocolate is that it can be molded into almost any shape. At Gertrude Hawk, special shapes add a sense of fun and playfulness to certain products.

Some fun shapes include solid chocolate beepers, chocolate calculators, chocolate remote controls—even a bouquet of chocolate roses! And, for the holidays, special chocolate pops are made in the shapes of snowmen and Santa Claus.

Above: *Special solid chocolate items.*
Below: *Snowmen pops.*

Chocolate Side-Bar

Gertrude's son, Elmer Hawk, says that Europeans and Americans like very different flavors in their chocolate. Europeans love hazelnut, praline, and marzipan (almond paste). Americans favor caramel, fruit flavors, and—above all—peanut butter.

Ready to Be Eaten

Each product is packed in a special kind of wrap, container, or box. Some chocolates are individually wrapped in foil before packaging. Others are placed in specially designed assortment boxes.

After the finished chocolates are collected and packaged, they get wrapped. Finished, wrapped boxes are placed in large shipping cartons and are sent out to thousands of hungry and very happy customers.

Glossary

Cocoa liquor the product of heating and grinding dried, cracked cacao beans.

Cylinder a shape with flat circular ends and sides shaped like the outside of a tube.

Ferment Aging process where natural yeasts begin to break down the enzymes in a food product.

Nib Soft, tasty inside of the cacao bean.

Pod a long casing that holds the seeds of certain plants.

Winnowing machine a device that separates material into usable and unusable piles.

For More Information

Books

Busenberg, Bonnie. *Vanilla, Chocolate, & Strawberry: The Story of Your Favorite Flavors.* Minneapolis, MN: Lerner Publications Co., 1994.

Jones, George. *My First Book of How Things Are Made: Crayons, Jeans, Guitars, Peanut Butter, and More* (Cartwheel Learning Bookshelf). New York, NY: Cartwheel Books, 1995.

Lewellyn, Claire. *Chocolate* (What's For Lunch). Danbury, CT: Children's Press, 1998.

Web Sites

Gertrude Hawk

Find out more about the chocolate made at Gertrude Hawk—www.gertrudehawk.com.

KidsCandy!

Test your candy knowledge—www.kidscandy.org.

Index